THE DEATH OF GOOD FORTUNE

A CHRISTMAS PLAY

BY
CHARLES WILLIAMS

Copyright © 2018 Read Books Ltd.
This book is copyright and may not be
reproduced or copied in any way without
the express permission of the publisher in writing

British Library Cataloguing-in-Publication Data
A catalogue record for this book is available from
the British Library

A HISTORY OF THE THEATRE

'The Theatre' is a collaborative form of fine art that uses live performers to present the experience of a real or imagined event. The performers may communicate this experience to the audience through combinations of gesture, speech, song, music, and dance, with elements of art, stagecraft and set design used to enhance the physicality, presence and immediacy of the experience. The specific place of the performance is also named by the word 'theatre' – derived from the Ancient Greek word *théatron*, meaning 'a place for viewing', itself from *theáomai*, meaning 'to see', 'watch' or 'observe'.

Modern Western theatre largely derives from ancient Greek drama, from which it borrows technical terminology, classification into genres, and many of its themes, stock characters, and plot elements. The city-state of Athens is where 'theatre' as we know it originated, as part of a broader culture of theatricality and performance in classical Greece that included festivals, religious rituals, politics, law, athletics, music, poetry, weddings, funerals, and symposia. Participation in the city-state's many festivals – and attendance at the City Dionysia as an audience member (or even as a participant in the theatrical productions) in particular, was an important part of citizenship.

The theatre of ancient Greece consisted of three types of drama: tragedy, comedy, and the satyr play (a form of tragicomedy, similar in spirit to the bawdy satire of burlesque). The origins of theatre in ancient Greece, according to Aristotle (384–322 BCE), the first theoretician of theatre, are to be found in the festivals that honoured Dionysus. These performances (the aforementioned City Dionysia) were held in semi-circular auditoria cut into hillsides, capable of seating 10,000–20,000 people. The stage consisted of a dancing floor (orchestra), dressing room and scene-building area (skene). Since the words were the most important part, good acoustics and clear delivery were paramount. The actors (always men) wore masks appropriate to the characters they represented, and each might play several parts.

Athenian tragedy (the oldest surviving form of tragedy) emerged sometime during the sixth century BCE, and flowered during the fifth century BCE – from the end of which it began to spread throughout the Greek world – and continued in popularity until the beginning of the Hellenistic period. Aeschylus, Sophocles, and Euripides were masters of the genre. The other side of the coin – Athenian comedy, is conventionally divided into three periods; 'Old Comedy', 'Middle Comedy', and 'New Comedy'. Old Comedy survives today largely in the form of the eleven surviving plays of Aristophanes, while Middle Comedy is largely lost (preserved only in a few relatively short fragments in authors such as Athenaeus of Naucratis). New Comedy is known primarily from the substantial papyrus fragments of Menander.

Western theatre developed and expanded considerably under the Romans. The theatre of ancient Rome was a thriving and diverse art form, ranging from festival performances of street theatre, nude dancing, and acrobatics, to the staging of Plautus's broadly appealing situation comedies, to the high-style, verbally elaborate tragedies of Seneca. Although Rome had a native tradition of performance, the Hellenization of Roman culture in the third century BCE had a profound and energizing effect on Roman theatre and encouraged the development of Latin literature of the highest quality for the stage. This tradition fed into the modern theatre we know today, and during the renaissance, theatre generally moved away from the poetic drama of the Greeks, and towards a more naturalistic prose style of dialogue. By the nineteenth century and the Industrial Revolution, this trend continued to progress.

In England, theatre was immensely popular, but took a big pause during 1642 and 1660 because of Cromwell's Interregnum. Prior to this, 'English renaissance theatre' was witnessed, with celebrated playwrights such as William Shakespeare, Christopher Marlowe and Ben Jonson. Under Queen Elizabeth, drama was a unified expression as far as social class was concerned, and the Court watched the same plays the commoners saw in the public playhouses. With the development of the private theatres, drama became more oriented towards the tastes and values of an upper-class audience however. By the later part of the reign of Charles I, few new plays were being written for the public theatres, which sustained themselves on the accumulated works of the previous decades. Theatre was now seen as something sinful and the Puritans tried very hard to drive it out of their society. Due to this stagnant period, once Charles II came back to the throne in 1660, theatre (among other arts) exploded with influences from France, and the wider continent.

The eighteenth century saw the widespread introduction of women to the stage – a development previously unthinkable. These women were looked at as celebrities (also a newer concept, thanks to ideas on individualism that were beginning to be born in Renaissance Humanism) but on the other hand, it was still very new and revolutionary. Comedies were full of the young and very much in vogue, with the storyline following their love lives: commonly a young roguish hero professing his love to the chaste and free minded heroine near the end of the play, much like Sheridan's *The School for Scandal*. Many of the comedies were fashioned after the French tradition, mainly Molière (the great comedic playwright), again harking back to the French influence of the King and his court after their exile.

After this point, there was an explosion of theatrical styles. Throughout the nineteenth century, the popular theatrical forms of Romanticism, melodrama, Victorian burlesque and the well-made plays of Scribe and Sardou gave way to the problem plays of Naturalism and Realism; the farces of Feydeau; Wagner's operatic *Gesamtkunstwerk*; musical theatre (including Gilbert and Sullivan's operas); F. C. Burnand's, W. S. Gilbert's and Wilde's drawing-room comedies; Symbolism; proto-Expressionism in the late works of August Strindberg and Henrik Ibsen; and Edwardian musical comedy. The list continues! These trends continued through the twentieth century in the realism of Stanislavski and Lee Strasberg, the political theatre of Erwin Piscator and Bertolt Brecht, the so-called Theatre of the Absurd of Samuel Beckett and Eugène Ionesco, and the rise of American and British musicals.

Theatre itself has an incredibly long history, and despite the massive proliferation of theatrical styles and mediums – it essentially owes its existence to the ancient Greeks and the Romans. The three main genres; tragedy, comedy and satyre, continue to influence plot themes, directing, writing and acting, with frequent and fascinating interrelations and overlaps. As a genre, it remains as popular today as it has ever been, and continues as a massive influence on popular culture more broadly. It is hoped that the current reader enjoys this book on the subject.

CHARLES WILLIAMS

Charles Walter Stansby Williams was born in London in 1886. He dropped out of University College London in 1904, and was hired by Oxford University Press as a proof-reader, quickly rising to the position of editor. While there, arguably his greatest editorial achievement was the publication of the first major English-language edition of the works of the Danish philosopher Søren Kierkegaard.

Williams began writing in the twenties and went on to publish seven novels. Of these, the best-known are probably *War in Heaven* (1930), *Descent into Hell* (1937), and *All Hallows' Eve* (1945) – all fantasies set in the contemporary world. He also published a vast body of well-received scholarship, including a study of Dante entitled *The Figure of Beatrice* (1944) which remains a standard reference text for academics today, and a highly unconventional history of the church, *Descent of the Dove* (1939). Williams garnered a number of well-known admirers, including T. S. Eliot, W. H. Auden and C. S. Lewis. Towards the end of his life, he gave lectures at Oxford University on John Milton, and received an honorary MA degree. Williams died almost exactly at the close of World War II, aged 58.

CHARACTERS

MARY
GOOD FORTUNE
THE KING
THE LOVER
THE MAGICIAN
THE OLD WOMAN
THE YOUTH
THE GIRL

The scene is an open place in a city

THE DEATH OF GOOD FORTUNE

MARY. Incipit vita nova: substance is love,
  love substance. Begins substance to move
  through everywhere the sensuality of earth and air.
  I was its mother in its beginning: I taught
  the royal soothsayers to follow a moving star,
  and brought them to their primal, far, and hierarchical Head.
  I am Wisdom whose name is Mary. I wept by the Dead.
  I arose with the Arisen. I see now
  where terribly through all spheres of gods and men
  pulse his ambiguous life and death dealing vibrations.
  His are all the alterations: and here shall be ours.
  There is on earth a being called Good Luck;
  he has spun much joy; his nature is heavenly,
  but when men fell, he was half-blinded;
  he does not know himself nor do men know him.
  I have determined that in this town this very day
  this gay popular lord shall come to his change
  and a strange new vision of himself; for now
  my lord my Son has made this clear—
  that all luck is good luck. And I,
  I struck by seven swords, witness too
  that all substance is love, all luck is good.
  Nor anywhere, for any flood of shed blood,
  sharp single anguish, or long languish of grief,
  shall any deny my word, or the great cry
  to every man upon earth of my lord your Son—
  all chance is heavenly, all luck is good.
  Let us see Good Fortune come now to his trance.
    [*She seats herself. The* OLD WOMAN *enters with a* YOUTH
THE OLD WOMAN. This is where the king will come; stay here.
THE YOUTH. Everything is gay this morning; see how the fair

THE DEATH OF GOOD FORTUNE

glows in the market: the tumblers calling and springing
and the jugglers flinging their quoits. I will go there
when we have seen the king. I will wrestle or cast
a hammer as fast and as far as their own champions.
I will be no puny challenger. Hey,
the blood runs quick this fair morning.
Will you speak to the king yourself, great aunt?

THE OLD WOMAN.   Yes.
They say that since his new guest came
the king will do all he is asked. I will task him little.
He could give me a house without hurting himself,
and will, I hope: there is good luck in the air.

THE YOUTH. And then I will go to the fair; I would fain see
the humped long-necked beast they call a camel
or a man fight, as they say he does naked,
with the wild long-toothed tiger from Seringapatam.

THE OLD WOMAN. Whatever you like.

THE YOUTH.   So I will. Who
is the king's new friend, to please him so?

THE OLD WOMAN. People like us do not know the lords' names,
only their acts. He came walking one day
into the city, under a bright sky,
himself as light and gay as that morning or this;
he was clearly a noble prince. Where he went
every event seemed better, every chance the happier.
That day I added to my store a piece of gold,
and all my neighbours told like good luck.

                             [*Enter the* LOVER *and the* MAGICIAN

THE LOVER. O but since he came, this king's friend,
this lord, this miracle-worker, even my fortune
seems to have grown greater. I love more,
and there is more joy in my more love.
There is a neat trick about the moments
that brings me to my sweet at any odd time

THE DEATH OF GOOD FORTUNE

when my heart is like to break not to see her.
THE MAGICIAN. It may well be: he says his name is Good Fortune.
THE LOVER. I can believe it indeed: he is all aerial.
O Good Fortune, be my god, and bless
me with her, and both of us with you.
THE MAGICIAN. He is like the full profession of my best art
gone out of itself into mankind.
We find too often the last prophecies are lost
at their end in a mist of faint knowledge. He,
this god—call you him so—at least this star,
came to the city in a dazzle. That I foresaw:
the law of the planets foretold a great event—
which must be he: unless beyond the bound
of all sidereal traffic, there were something more—
but that no astrology has ever found.
THE OLD WOMAN. Sir, will the king come soon?
THE LOVER. Soon.
THE MAGICIAN. Nay, it seems no one even waits now:
lo, the king, and—do we say a star?
THE LOVER. Star or daemon—call him our god Good Fortune.
   [*The* KING *enters with* GOOD FORTUNE, *the* MAGICIAN's
   daughter attending]
THE KING. This city, that holds all our lives,
thrives well; but now you are come,
our lord Good Fortune, it has a spell within it
to be fortunate for ever; strangers shall see and say
how our devotion praises in the phases of its passage
only you; to you is all our homage.
Here we rule best and love best;
here knowledge finds wisdom and age rest.
Happy are you, Good Fortune, and we in you.
Deign only to maintain your grace in this place.
GOOD FORTUNE. I am Good Fortune, satisfaction, the action of the
heart

when all goes well. I have made this your city
my divine choice; mine while I care to stay—
and I think now I shall not leave you; I
have a power of fidelity too, and it may be true
that I shall stay here and enjoy you; your town
shall be known everywhere for a nest of young delight,
a camp of successful joys, and a rest for the old.
I am always young, a giver of good things,
and you here, by my mere arbitrary choice,
I deign to gratify; cry then my praise;
no god is stronger than I except Pan,
and Pan and I have divided the world between us.

MARY. It is known everywhere that Pan is already dying,
for the substance of love takes him with great shocks;
and you too, fair lord, shall find what locks
were broken for ever when my Son strode through hell.

THE KING. It is true; my armies, since you came, win
on all my frontiers; where my enemies entered in,
they are thrown back; victory is mine alone.
I have good chance now to reward good service.

THE OLD WOMAN. My husband's blood being shed then for you
in one of your fights, and he dead, great sir,
grant me the reward of his service; grant me a house
for old bones to lie securely. No alms;
only my own roof. I have saved; it lies
hidden in my lodging, but the lodging is dank and rank
with the smells of the butchers' quarter. I would rather live
in the new houses you, my king, have built
beyond the river: besides, now I live
with my son and his wife; we cannot get on together.
She is young and bitter and I am old and tired.
My husband died for you; give me now
a proper lodging where I can live on my savings.

THE KING. Willingly; take which you choose: our lord here

smiles on all petitions, and I allow,
I would do also anything for my friends here
but they do not need it; their ends are beyond me:
yours is in your maid and yours in your art.
Yet my heart is apt to give: is there none?
and you?

THE GIRL. Nothing.

THE MAGICIAN.   Nothing?

THE GIRL.   What else?
Can you, father, or your new god Good Luck
help me in a world where despair only is true?
No; if that is a god, I am an atheist.
I will wait a little to see if your god will die.

GOOD FORTUNE. Do you say, girl, that I am bound to die?

THE GIRL. I say I do not believe in you; nothing more.

GOOD FORTUNE. Look round; see them happy; will not you be?
Worship me, and see what I can do.

THE GIRL. I have lived long enough on earth to know
that earth has no new birth of good luck.

GOOD FORTUNE. But I am not of earth; I am aerial,
born in the mid heavens, a prince of the zodiac,
heir to fine fantasies, lacking nothing.
Will you take them as a gift?

THE GIRL.   No; they exist nowhere.
They are the twist of man's heart to defend itself.
You may come from the middle air, but you are deceit
if you do; your feet have no print on our soil.

MARY. He is deceit indeed, but only because
he does not know how great a prince he is.
Since my Son died, all things are good luck,
and fate and good luck and heaven are one name.

GOOD FORTUNE. Am I defrauded in my chosen town?

ALL THE OTHER PERSONS.   No.
Lord, she is obstinate, false, heretical;

THE DEATH OF GOOD FORTUNE

 she will stick at nothing to make herself great:
abate displeasure; treasure us instead.
THE KING. Cense we now, in divine ritual, this godhead.
THE LOVER. Tread we the circle; beat we the solemn vow.
THE YOUTH [*to the* OLD WOMAN]. Shall we go?
THE OLD WOMAN.   We cannot.
THE YOUTH.   Why? the fair waits.
 Must we stand by while the king ceremonializes?
let's to the prizes! let's to the loud noise!
THE OLD WOMAN. Hist! you will do better if you worship the god.
      [*The ceremony of censing; during which—*
MARY. Before the advent of the necromantic kings
 in the beginning, I saw a star sliding,
shining, guiding their god-divining caravan.
Its name was called *TYXH*, its flame was fortune,
its messenger and shape on earth was this lord here,
whose sphere above attended my Son's birth;
but he, being blinded by cloud, is half-minded
to glorify himself for only half his worth;
I must teach him all: it is time that he should die.
GOOD FORTUNE. Ah! . . . rocks the earth, or was it I?
THE KING. God, what frightened you?
GOOD FORTUNE.   What lightened then
 or did my eyes dazzle?
        [*He leans on the* LOVER
THE LOVER.   Your hand is cold !
 what is the matter, our God?
GOOD FORTUNE.   My head splits!
THE OLD WOMAN. You have cramp in the stomach, or else the
  damp airs
of the valley have given you a chill.
GOOD FORTUNE.   My spirit is flung
 into fits of terror!

THE DEATH OF GOOD FORTUNE

THE MAGICIAN. He is rigid in a seizure.
GOOD FORTUNE. Ah!
[*He falls*

THE KING. You—look! what ails him?
THE MAGICIAN. I did not dare
even to fear this—
THE GIRL. But I—I knew.
THE YOUTH. Come; you promised; let us get to the fair.
Our lords die; are we to cry their wake?
Take we a quiet—
THE OLD WOMAN. I am afraid! hush!
Be quiet yourself, you fool!
THE MAGICIAN. Must I look?
Must I think that this god can die?
Must I think that a secretly-sliding star
that the gods neglect has struck this lord of Good Luck?
When that hiding opens—
[*He kneels by him and stands up*
He is dead.
THE OLD WOMAN. Dead?
THE KING. He—*he* dead?
THE YOUTH. All the fair has stopped! what has happened?
THE LOVER. This god cannot die.
THE MAGICIAN. So? And yet he is dead.
[*They all stare at* GOOD FORTUNE; *then they look at each other*
And what will happen now?
THE GIRL. O woe!
I did not quite believe it!
THE LOVER. But if Good Fortune
is dead . . .
THE OLD WOMAN. The money! the money I hid away
to spend on my own living, and save my head
from having at last to lie in a bed lent

by my son's wife grudgingly till I died....
Come!
THE YOUTH. But the fair?
THE OLD WOMAN. Curse the fair! Come.
[*She hurries him out*
THE LOVER. If Good Fortune is dead, what will happen to love?
THE MAGICIAN. What indeed?
THE KING. To the Kingdom?
THE MAGICIAN. What indeed?
THE LOVER. The city, he said, is a place of youth; if Good Fortune ... and how much is truth a part of Good Fortune?
THE GIRL. Not at all: that I do know: not at all.
[*He stares at her and rushes out*
THE MAGICIAN. Sir, will you not also hurry to see about the frontiers? are no fears growing in you?
THE KING. Yes.
[*He begins to go, and returns*
Do you try first: can you spy by your tables of magic the truth of this? Try.
THE MAGICIAN. My art was my heart, as her savings and his love and your royalty were hearts' realms too; it is sped if this lord of fortunate chances is indeed dead.
THE GIRL. Father—
THE MAGICIAN. Hush! If your atheism was right, plight yourself to it, but do not now speak.
THE KING. Try.
THE MAGICIAN. I will try—to please you, and to satisfy myself that what I feared might come has come.
[*He lifts his wand*
I lift the hazel rod in the banishing pentagram against the god of illusion, against Lilith the accurst: depart, incubi and succubi! depart, phantoms; I call on the stars of heaven in their even rule,

THE DEATH OF GOOD FORTUNE

exact powers, to show me the fact happening.
Show me the measured fate of this kingdom: show!

                                                 [*He speaks to the* KING
Your enemies move on your borders; in the front line
your orders are frustrated; one of your towns is on fire;
your reserves are belated in the forest. This god
shall be waited on soon by many men,
and your kingdom be past and your crown given to another,
because the curse of the death of Good Luck is come, and . . .

                                                          [*He tries to see*

THE KING. Look; look forward but a month!
THE MAGICIAN. Good Luck is dead: I can see nothing
  beyond this moment, the moment of his death.
THE KING. A week—nay, a day; see but a day;
  see if I can hold them back but so many hours—
THE MAGICIAN. Do you think that your powers of war are to be the
    only
sons of luck? is the haft of your kingdom more
than the craft of my mind? I see nothing; do you hear?
I who beheld—what did I then behold?
infinity? yes, except for one star
that was always moving there, and never where
my art expected. Here are your other friends—
back so soon? It seems something ends
their plenilunary content.

                                  [*The* OLD WOMAN *returns; she is crying*
THE OLD WOMAN. Thieves! thieves!
My house was broken open and my floor dug up—
· my money was gone: send, sir, some guard
to take the thieves. I am a poor woman
and had hoped to have peace in my last days.
Send someone to hunt the thieves, my king.
THE KING. You are not like to have peace, nor I neither.
Something more will be here soon to strike.

THE OLD WOMAN. What do I care if your enemies share your
   crown?
I shall wait until they pass; the grass that grows
in a palace gate finds soil too poor at a hut's.
All that I need is freedom from my son's wife.
                                  [*The* LOVER *enters*
THE MAGICIAN. And your life, young man?
                        [*The* LOVER *looks at him terribly*
                                        It began well.
Who would have thought the death of a god could change
what (it seemed) fell beyond the gods?
THE LOVER. Be still: he said right; this is a city of youth.
THE MAGICIAN. Love is kind to youth.
THE LOVER.   Love is . . . old man,
take care; the heir of love is a torn heart.
THE GIRL. Were you happy?
THE LOVER. Happy? We were fortunate and therefore happy.
But you knew better.
THE GIRL.   Are you sure of that?
THE KING. If indeed Good Fortune is now dead,
our god, our only hope, behoves all
to put away our loves, and what may fall
take nobly, to make a nucleus of hearts
resigned with one mind against Fate
to share what we have, and in natural honour brave
all else. Resign yourselves; be strong.
THE LOVER. Sir, that is nonsense; that is the talk
of men who believed once that loss might occur.
Never was I of those. Woes might be,
but this is more than grief, and yet belief
rages in me, delirious but unable to die.
Good Fortune may be dead for you, but for me
his spirit roars here, demanding godhead,
nay, having it: I will not be resigned.

THE DEATH OF GOOD FORTUNE

THE KING. What will you do then?
THE LOVER.   I do not know what I will do.
   But I will not be content; it is all untrue,
   this content, this resignation: love must live,
   and if a woman coils up in another's heart
   and spoils love's accidents, love's substance must gather head,
   I do not see how, but somehow: love must live.
THE KING. That he could do while Good Fortune lived.
   But I must lose my crown now, and why
   should you show less content? all the earth
   is resigned: why should a lover's mind escape?
THE LOVER. Because his love is more substantial than yours.
                                  [*To the* MAGICIAN
   Master, though your knowledge fails, you are not unwise.
   Which of us two is true?
THE MAGICIAN. Either; go you
   living in death and he dying in life.
   Toss for your choice.
THE KING.   Which did the stars say
   was the wiser? which is the power in your own mind?
THE MAGICIAN. Give me your hands; there is much power in the
     hand.
   My predecessors say that all enchantment
   is summed in the free hand; therefore a priest
   fetches blessing out of the air with his,
   or a woman stretches hers to love and be loved
   with the palm's inward: give them; if the gods die,
   let us see, wherever rage and resignation endure,
   what cure there may be.
                                  [*He takes their hands*
                Now the shrouded battle
   in my brain halts; I see the unclouded stars
   sitting still, as if they were the will of Nature,
   of substance the creature. I see, between two skies,

the great stars, the million hints of perfection,
stretching far away, and I see the moving star,
spending its glory everywhere, and not losing,
descending: is it devising to earth—and here?
It is coming down; the earth is drenched with it;
blenched on high, its great companions sit,
fit to be watchers of fate, but not fate;
fate is the stolen gold and the false love
and the lost battle, in the death of all good fortune.
Hold yourselves; veil yourselves; the core
of the moving star shoots at my back; who
waits in this city to be clothed with the star?
                              [*He whirls round on* MARY
Woman, by the star that glides into your frame,
by the path that Nature hides from all wizards,
by the wrath and the resignation of death, speak!
                              [MARY *remains silent*
Mother of the only moving star, speak!
Mother of disaster, mother of destiny, speak!
Mother, if you are a mother at all, speak!
                              [*He falls on his knees*
MARY. I will speak because you know of what I speak:
you, wizard, though you do not reach it, know.
But tell me first what you think you wish to know.
THE MAGICIAN. It can only be spoken under great veils,
since it is we who must be what we wish to know:
when all fails, what is the right thing to be?
MARY. You must be as you can. I say only, when all fails,
then is the time, brother, to work a little.
THE OLD WOMAN. No work will fetch me my warm room
where I can be alone or ask who I like.
I worked once; now I want to rest;
how can I rest in my son's wife's house?
MARY. My own Son sent me to live in another's.

THE DEATH OF GOOD FORTUNE

I have no mother's word for any woman,
sister, beyond this terrible biting word.
THE KING. Tell us this difficult biting word.
MARY.   No;
biting but not difficult; quite simple.
When your god Good Fortune dies, the only thing
is to bid your god Good Fortune rise again.
THE OLD WOMAN. That is silly.
THE KING.   That is impossible.
THE LOVER.   That is true.
THE GIRL. O do not say so, do not say so; I know it is true.
THE MAGICIAN. Do it.
MARY.   It is a great risk you run.
You may not, when it is done, much believe it.
THE THREE MEN. If it can be done, we can believe it.
MARY.   Can you?
We shall see; I will do it anywhere for any who ask—
on seas or in cities; wherever Good Fortune dies,
there am I to bid him rise, if you will,
after his proper manner.
    [*She goes to the body and touches it; then she stretches her hand over it*]
Good Fortune, god Good Fortune, do you hear?
                                [*She pauses*
Good Fortune, dead Good Fortune, do you hear?
GOOD FORTUNE [*in a dead voice*]. I hear; all the dead shake before you.
MARY. Where are you?
GOOD FORTUNE.   In a dry place, between two skies.
MARY. Go forward. . . . Where are you?
GOOD FORTUNE. Among millions of stars;
it is difficult here even for the ghost of a god
to move forward, as my substance makes me move.

THE DEATH OF GOOD FORTUNE

MARY. Sparks of perfection, shining hints of perfection;
between the hints, sparks, and slivers of perfection,
go forward.... Where are you?
GOOD FORTUNE. Dying in death.
THE LOVER [*murmuring*]. That is it! that is it! that is where I am
now.
MARY. Where are you?
GOOD FORTUNE. Under a shape crucified and burning.
MARY. Go forward.... Where are you?
GOOD FORTUNE. Your voice is behind and before me.
I am before you; you are on a throne.
A child is standing on your knee; a small hand
blesses everything, though nothing but I am there.
It is marked with a dark ring of dried blood.
MARY. What does he say?
GOOD FORTUNE. He says: 'Live, Good Fortune'—
woman, woman on earth, tell me to die.
MARY. What is he doing?
GOOD FORTUNE. He has taken my heart from my side,
and is twisting it in his hands.
MARY. Untwisting.

[*She pauses*

Live; do not sleep; tell us what he says.
GOOD FORTUNE [*moaning*]. O... he says: 'Good Fortune, you have
your fortune;
yours is the only fortune; all luck is good.'
THE LOVER. That is it! that is it! all luck is good.
Why did you tell me to be resigned? Fool!
Why did no one tell me?—all luck is good.
THE GIRL. Dare you say it?
THE LOVER. Dare you not believe it? up!
bear up with me and say that luck is blessed.
THE MAGICIAN. This is the track of the single moving star,
between motionless stars: all luck is blessed.

THE DEATH OF GOOD FORTUNE

THE KING. How is it true there is no evil fortune?
  it is evil fortune to lose my crown and my head.
THE OLD WOMAN. To be bullied by my own son and nagged by his wife;
  it is silly to call that kind of luck good.
MARY. It is done; you must make your own choice now
  and show as you will. Live, Good Fortune, live.
  Live and return and tell us what you know.
GOOD FORTUNE. How shall I be able to tell you what I know?
  I found myself riding through the heavens; below,
  on earth, wise men were riding to a Birth,
  to a lonely, difficult, universal gospel
  of the nature, its nature and all things' nature.
  The star in which I stood was moving to a loving
  between the Mother and the Child, and as I saw
  I became other than I was and a new creature;
  I was the master of all chances; all chances
  made the multiple star in which I rode.
  Therefore it shone, and now I take a new name
  that came when the Child smiled for the sake of its Mother:
  I will be called Blessed Luck for ever;
  the temples fall; and all kinds of fate:
  blessed is the Nature and the Fortune in the minds of men.
  Who among you all has professed me now?
  who moves with me to welcome all chances that may come?
THE MAGICIAN. This I know, if I do not believe: here am I.
THE LOVER [*to the* GIRL]. Say.
THE GIRL.   Say for me.
THE LOVER.   I will say for both—
  this we believe, if we do not know: here are we.
THE OLD WOMAN [*to the* KING]. Will you agree?
THE KING. Why should I agree?
  I think it makes sense and I think it does not;

15

THE DEATH OF GOOD FORTUNE

if I have found defeat is there no defence
less wild than this?

THE OLD WOMAN. And how can I agree
when I think my child hates to have me there,
my own son, and I nowhere else to go?

[*She screams out*

You! Stop! what do you say it all means?
I only ask common honesty in the gods.
Do you say, you fellow who pretended to die,
that whatever happens to me is equal good fortune?

GOOD FORTUNE. Yes.

THE OLD WOMAN. It means nothing to me.

THE KING. Something
perhaps, but nothing I have any hope to be.

[*They turn to go*

MARY. Sister, only those whose hearts are broken
might at a pinch blame you, but not here.
Brother, if you will not push to the last inch
your knowledge of defeat, you must keep your heart unspoken.
But these here, they have to make the choice
or to know, at the very least, that the choice exists.
You have chosen your ways; be blessed; go with God.

[*To the others*]

And you, great ones, you must always make your choice,
or always, at least, know that the choice exists—
all luck is good—or not; even when the ninth
step is nine times as difficult as the first.

[*To the audience*]

And you—this has been sung a long time
among you, as among the cities your companions—
Antioch, Alexandria, Bologna, Paris, Oxford.
Substance moves in you; my lord your Son
loves you; choose your ways. Go with God.

[*They go out*

www.ingramcontent.com/pod-product-compliance
Lightning Source LLC
Chambersburg PA
CBHW031819110426
42743CB00057B/1074